essentials

Develop a Winning
Marketing Plan

Time-saving books that teach specific skills to busy people, focusing on what really matters; the things that make a difference – the *essentials*.

Other books in the series include:

Boost Your Word Power

Expand Your Vocabulary

Buying a Franchise

Leading Teams

Making the Most of Your Time

Solving Problems

Coaching People

Hiring People

Making Great Presentations

Writing Good Reports

The Ultimate Business Plan

Writing Business E-mails

For full details please send for a free copy of the latest catalogue.
See back cover for address.

Develop a Winning Marketing Plan

Phil Stone

ESSENTIALS

Published in 2001 by
How To Books Ltd, 3 Newtec Place,
Magdalen Road, Oxford OX4 1RE, United Kingdom
Tel: (01865) 793806   Fax: (01865) 248780
email: info@howtobooks.co.uk
www.howtobooks.co.uk

British Library Cataloguing in Publication Data
A catalogue record for this book is available from
the British Library

Edited by Francesca Mitchell
Cover design by Shireen Nathoo Design, London
Produced for How To Books by Deer Park Productions
Designed and typeset by Shireen Nathoo Design, London
Printed and bound in Great Britain by
Bell & Bain Ltd., Glasgow

NOTE: The material contained in this book is set out in good faith for
general guidance and no liability can be accepted for loss or expense
incurred as a result of relying in particular circumstances on statements
made in the book. The laws and regulations are complex and liable to
change, and readers should check the current position with the relevant
authorities before making personal arrangements.

ESSENTIALS *is an imprint of*
How To Books

Contents

Preface

Many businesses do not understand the importance of a marketing plan. This is a fundamental mistake. Marketing is relevant to all businesses, no matter what size, and you ignore it at your peril.

The core function of marketing is to identify what customers want and then to satisfy that desire. Unless you understand what customers want there is little chance of you being able to satisfy their demands. The simple point is that if you have no customers you have no business.

Marketing is not a difficult exercise. Whilst many of the management tools used in marketing can seem complicated they are actually simple to understand. They are there to provide a structured framework for you to use to present your marketing plan in a logical format.

A marketing plan will help you gain an understanding of the market and identify where you have a competitive advantage. This will enable you to set clear objectives as to where you want your business to be in the future. You can then decide on the strategies to use to exploit the opportunities available to you and achieve

your overall business goals. Without clear focus
and direction your business is going nowhere.

Phil Stone

1 Before You Start

Satisfying customer demand is the primary aim of marketing.
To do that you must understand the market.

In this chapter four things that really matter:

~ **Understanding marketing**

~ **Why you need a marketing plan**

~ **Considering marketing and business objectives**

~ **Compiling the mission statement**

Marketing is all about finding out what your customers want and satisfying that need. For many small businesses the whole concept of marketing is a minefield of jargon and they therefore avoid it. It is often confused with sales, but without adequate marketing there may be no sales. Unless you can establish exactly what the market is demanding, where it should be supplied, and at what price, you may have no customers.

A marketing plan is often confused with a business plan. The two are quite distinct and have different purposes. A marketing plan is an internal document that sets out a detailed analysis of the market and the marketing strategy to be employed. A business plan considers the whole business environment and sets out the strategy for the business. Whilst there will be a marketing section within the business plan it will not, and indeed should not, be as detailed as the marketing plan. *

Is this you?

Marketing, that's the same as sales isn't it? • I don't have time for marketing, I've got a business to run. • Why do I need a marketing plan anyway, I've already got a business plan? • What's the difference between business objectives and marketing objectives, surely they must be the same? • A mission statement – that just sounds like marketing jargon to me.

* Some businesses are successful purely because they are in the right place at the right time. Most businesses, however, need to plan their marketing if they are to succeed.

Understanding marketing

Marketing is not a new concept. Since the early days of trading, businesses have had to supply the right product, at the right price, in the right place. Marketing merely brings all these essential elements together into a formalised structure. There is nothing difficult about the processes and tools used in marketing. They may have complicated names, but the actual tools themselves are easy to understand and to use.

You should also be clear that marketing is not the same as selling. There is often great confusion between these two words. Some businesses have both a marketing director and a sales director, other businesses have either a sales director or a marketing director. In all cases they have entirely different functions.

The marketing director will be responsible for planning the strategic marketing of the business. The sales director will more than likely be responsible for a field sales team. *

* You must understand that sales are the end result of successful marketing. Without a comprehensive marketing plan there could be no sales.

The key point with marketing is that it is a matching process. It matches the businesses capabilities with the needs of the consumer. To do that you must first of all establish exactly what it is that your business does. You can then gain an understanding of the market that you are in.

Many businesses claim they have no time for marketing. They have a product that sells and that is all they need. This is a very short-sighted approach. Consumer demand can be very fickle and change overnight without warning, so the whole concept of marketing is to keep up to date with what is happening in the market.

This means that marketing will include all of the following factors:

~ the name of your business

~ the name of your products or services

~ the design and presentation of your products or service

~ the methods of manufacture or servicing

~ the prices that you will charge

Promote

plan

~ the advertising and promotion that you will undertake

~ the location of your business

The whole concept of marketing should be seen as a continuous cycle. It starts with the basic idea for generating an income and it finishes when sales have been made and you arrive back at the start again. It is never a straight-line process. To stay ahead of your competitors your marketing must be ongoing, with new ideas and fresh income streams.

Why you need a marketing plan

The only way that you can clarify your marketing aims and objectives is by formulating a marketing plan. This will also force you to examine the threats and opportunities that you may encounter in the market. It may seem a difficult and unnecessary task but it is an essential element of the overall business planning process. *

It is important that you understand why a marketing plan is different from the marketing section of your business plan. If you have a sole product or service the marketing section of your business plan may be similar to your marketing plan. A good marketing plan will, however, reveal a more in-depth analysis of the market, together with details of the marketing strategies to be adopted.

If your business involves a number of products or services it is generally recommended that you have a separate marketing plan for each segmented product or service. Your business plan will then merely incorporate a summary of the market analysis for each segment together with an overview of your marketing strategy.

Even if you only have one product or service, an updated marketing plan is vital if you are considering changing your marketing strategy. Unless you complete a full and up-to-date analysis of the market

* *A marketing plan will allow you to gain ground on your competitors and help you channel your marketing activities in the right direction.*

you cannot be sure that your new strategy will succeed. For example, if you are considering price changes or the offer of discounts, you must evaluate the consequences of such actions before you implement them.

There are four essential reasons why you need a marketing plan:

~ You need to establish exactly what products or services you are selling. This should be completed in sufficient detail to actually mean something and not be just a bland description.

~ You need to identify who your customers are. Link your customers to your product base and segment them into key groups. The intention is to target most of your resources at the most profitable of the specific segments.

~ You need to find out why your customers buy from you. In many ways this is the most important factor. It will clearly define their needs and wants as consumers and from this you can structure your future marketing strategy.

~ You need to establish what differentiates your business from others of a similar nature. You need to establish why it is your customers buy from you instead of your competitors. It is essential that you distinguish yourself with a unique selling point.

A good marketing plan is essential to answer three basic questions in terms of the market as a whole. Where are you now? Where do you want to be? How you are going to get there? In simple terms – marketing audit, marketing objectives, marketing strategy.

An effective marketing plan is an essential tool in the business planning process. The plan itself will not guarantee success in the market but the lack of one will offer you no assistance at all. You must plan your activities if you wish to exploit your businesses capabilities to the full. *

Considering marketing and business objectives

It is essential that marketing objectives are not confused with business objectives. Business objectives set the direction for the future and relate to your business as a whole. They are the principle objectives of your business. Marketing objectives, however, are secondary objectives. Your marketing objectives and the strategy you will use cannot be formulated until the overall objectives and strategies of your business have been defined.

On this basis your marketing objectives must be consistent with your business objectives. They must also be compatible with the direction of your business set out in your business plan. The marketing objectives should also be **SMART**.

SMART is an acronym for:

Specific
Measurable
Agreed
Realistic
Timed

In all cases, marketing objectives will flow from the broad business objectives and will need to be translated into key areas. These key areas will be vital to the success of your business – for example, increasing market penetration. You must remember that primary marketing objectives can only relate to products and markets. They should not be confused with objectives relating to price or promotional methods that are entirely subservient.

There are four alternatives that you can think about when considering your marketing objectives:

~ selling existing products to existing markets

~ extending existing products into new markets

~ developing new products for existing markets

~ developing new products for new markets.

This framework is known as the Ansoff matrix. The use of this tool, and other methods by which marketing objectives can be established, is covered in more detail in Chapter 3, Establishing Your Marketing Objectives *

Compiling the mission statement

Your marketing plan must start with a mission statement. Sometimes called a *vision* statement, it should detail the whole purpose of the business and under normal circumstances should consist of no more than one page. In many ways it is the hardest part of the marketing plan to formulate. It is also the most misunderstood part of the plan itself.

* Objectives within a marketing plan will be many and varied. They must be expressed in a clear and simple manner and be easily measurable. Vague objectives will only lead to confusion over the direction your business needs to take.

One of the worst examples of a mission statement that I have seen simply had four words, 'To be the best'. This told me absolutely nothing of what the business was about. What did they want to be best at? How were they going to achieve it? Perhaps of more importance, how would they know when they had actually achieved it?

There are four key components of a Mission Statement:

~ The role or contribution that the business makes – is it a voluntary organisation or a charity? Are you in business to supply goods and services and make a profit?

~ A definition of the business – this should be given in terms of the benefits you provide or the needs that you satisfy. It should not define what you do or what you make. These should have been outlined as part of the first component.

~ An outline of your distinctive competencies – the factors that differentiate your business from the competition. These will be the skills or capabilities that you offer that are not, or cannot be, offered by your competitors.

~ The indications for the future – what the business will do, what it might do in the future and what it will never do.

Formulating your mission statement is not easy and this is largely because it is philosophical and qualitative in nature.

Unfortunately, this can also mean that the mission statement becomes either unnecessarily broad or restrictively narrow simply because its true value is not understood.

In some cases it actually bears no resemblance to the business it is supposed to describe and can even consist of nothing other than pompous and moral statements. These are of no value whatsoever. A mission statement will require considerable thought if it is to convey the right message.

It is also essential that it be easily understood and communicated to employees and customers alike. Treat it like the historic family motto or heraldic shield. It should represent the business's core values and as such all people associated with the business should feel proud of it.

Summary points

★ Make sure that you understand that marketing is not the same as selling.

★ You must have a separate internal marketing plan as distinct from the marketing section of your business plan.

★ Do not confuse marketing objectives with business objectives. They must be distinctive but they must also be consistent with each other.

★ Use the mission statement to set out your core business values. Make sure that it is clear and concise and communicated to employees and customers alike.

2 Completing the Marketing Audit

The marketing audit is the foundation on which you will build your strategy. Without a firm foundation your strategy will not succeed.

In this chapter five things that really matter:

~ **Establishing your market and customers**
~ **Defining your products**
~ **Considering price**
~ **Evaluating promotion methods**
~ **Being in the right place**

A successful marketing plan can only be based on the results of a comprehensive audit of the market. Unless you know who your customers are likely to be, how much they will pay and where they will buy, you cannot formulate a successful strategy. You must also remember that although you may have a distinctive and innovative product, unless people know about it they cannot purchase it.

The key to a successful marketing audit is segmentation. You must segment your customers and the market into identifiable groups that are differentiated from each other. This may be done using demographic factors, geographical factors, or be based on product usage.

Once you have clearly defined the market or markets that you are in and defined your target customer groups you can then complete the audit. The final part of the audit will look at the pricing and promotion techniques used by competitors in the market and also your physical location. *

* Segmentation of the market is not easy but it does have tangible benefits. Unless you understand who is buying from you, and why, your final marketing strategy may be focused in entirely the wrong direction.

Is this you?

I don't need an audit of the market, I know the products I have so all I need to do is sell them. • I don't care about the competition, I can beat them all on price alone. • Promotion will be easy, I'll advertise in the same places my competitors do. If it works for them it will work for me. • Location is not important, customers will buy from me wherever I am.

Establishing your market and customers

Segmentation is the most important factor when looking at your potential market and customers. It is essential that you categorise your market and your customers into groups that all contain the same broad characteristics. Whilst it can be difficult to actually segment your customers into distinct groups, if you use the following as a guide to segmentation it will offer some assistance.

~ Segments must be of a suitable size in comparison with the overall market. There is little point in establishing a segment that represents a small percentage of your overall customers.

~ The customers within each segment must be similar in nature but at the same time be entirely distinct from other customers.

~ Within each segment you must be able to establish which customers are buying what products and why these customers are buying a particular product.

~ The customers within the segment must be accessible. You must establish whether you will be able to reach, communicate with, and, more importantly, sell to the customers within that segment.

When considering the segmentation of your market you will undoubtedly encounter a fascinating phenomenon. You will discover that it is only a small percentage of your customers who account for a large percentage of your sales. This phenomenon is known as the 'Pareto' effect or the 80/20 rule. Conversely it also means that a large percentage of your customers account for a small percentage of your sales.

It is extremely important that you understand that you should not ignore those customers who make a minimal contribution to sales. By establishing their needs and segmenting them properly they could become a potential source of increased business. *

By the same token, you cannot ignore the small percentage of customers who provide the bulk of your sales. You cannot afford to lose these customers for they will obviously have a significantly greater impact on your sales volume. The most crucial aspect of segmentation is that it will give you the ability to identify the needs and wants of all your customers. You can then use this information later on when considering your objectives and your strategy.

There is, of course, another aspect of the market audit that needs to be considered and that is the identification of your competitors. It is just as important to have available all the information on your competitors as it is to have information on your existing or potential customers. If you do not know what your competitors are doing there is little prospect of you being

It could be that your customers purchase from your competitors because you do not supply certain products within your product range. If you can meet their needs they may prefer to purchase from you.

able to compete. It is essential therefore that you obtain the following information:

~ product range in terms of specification and price

~ availability of discounts

~ delivery arrangements

~ terms of trade, i.e. cash or credit.

Some of this information may already be available to you if you have an existing connection or have been previously employed in the same industry. If, however, you are a potential new entrant to the market, you may find during your market research into potential customers that some of them may be customers of your competitor. They can therefore pass on information about the service they receive.

Once you have gained as much information as you can, a SWOT analysis will put it into a logical form. The use of a SWOT analysis is covered in Chapter 3. *

* You must know who your customers are and what they want. Without that information you may have no customers.

Defining your products

You can only define your products when you have established what it is your potential customers wish to purchase. Returning yet again to one of the core aspects of marketing – matching what your customers want to what it is that you sell. When considering your audit you must also look at the lifecycle of your products and establish exactly where they are within that cycle. There are five phases in the product lifecycle:

~ introduction

~ growth

~ maturity

~ saturation

~ decline

A technique that you can employ to define your products is known as the 'BCG matrix'. This matrix classifies your products according to cash usage and cash generation compared with relative market share and growth rate.

'Star' products – these have a high market share and high growth rate. They also generate a large cash inflow, although this is fully offset by the cash they require for production.	'Question Mark' products – these have a high growth rate although they only have a low market share. Cash generated is minimal against cash used, the net cashflow is negative.
'Cash Cow' products – these have a high market share although a low potential growth rate. They generate a high cash inflow against minimal cash required for production.	'Dog' products – these have a low market share and low potential growth rate. They generate minimal cash inflow which is fully matched by the cash they require for production.

To expand a little further on these product definitions:

~ 'Question Mark' products have not yet achieved a dominant market position with the associated large cashflow. They could also be products that have slipped back from a previous dominant position. They are high users of cash because they are in the growth stage of the product lifecycle.

~ 'Star' products have achieved a high market share and in general terms will be entirely self-financing in terms of cashflow. They will probably be new products in terms of lifecycle.

~ 'Cash Cow' products are market leaders and whilst there is little potential growth they are normally in a stable market. In lifecycle terms they are at maturity or entering saturation.

~ 'Dog' products have little or no future and in lifecycle terms they are in decline.

From all of the above you can see that, following introduction into the market, the product lifecycle is represented in chronological order by 'Question Marks', 'Stars', and then 'Cash Cows'. In cash terms, the cash generated by the 'Cash Cows' is used to invest in the 'Stars' and a select few from the 'Question Marks'.

This becomes part of the process of product management and is covered in more detail in Chapter 4. For the moment, however, it is important that you also understand the potential dangers of misusing the BCG matrix. When conducting your product audit, you may find that a large number of products are in low growth markets, i.e. 'Dog' products. It is essential therefore that you establish the relationship that such products have within the overall market.

The BCG matrix is an ideal tool for evaluating your products and establishing their place in the lifecycle process. It does not, however, take into account profitability and this dimension needs to be considered when defining your products.

It may be that one such product could have been the initial product introduced by you that established your brand name and reputation in the market. It would be very unwise to remove that product from your product range even if it does now only have a low market share. It is more than likely that if it is a manufactured product it will share the same production and distribution facilities with other new products. As such, despite the low market share, it will still remain a profitable product. *

Considering price

It is important to remember that price does not always play a large part in the purchase decision by customers. It should also be emphasised that at this stage you are not yet considering your future pricing strategy. This will be looked at in detail in Chapter 4. You are still at the audit stage and therefore the price considerations that need to be looked at are the market comparisons.

This is an essential part of your research and all too often is actually missed at the marketing audit stage of the planning process. When you looked at your competitors in the first part of this chapter you should have gained details of the prices that they charge. You should also have established what discounts, if any, they offer and under what terms.

The importance of this is to give you a clear understanding of what pricing decisions are being taken by your competitors in the market. You will also need to link this information to the product lifecycle analysis that you completed earlier. For example, a low price charged by a competitor could represent a 'Question Mark' product that is being priced accordingly to increase market share.

It may be that you have no intention of competing in the market purely on price. What is important is that you have a clear perception of the pricing structures within the market. This will then give you the opportunity of competing on different terms, for example on quality, which may also command a higher base price in the market.

As part of the audit you will also have to look at costs. This is, of course, the other side of the price equation that will ultimately reflect on profitability. If you can produce the same product as your competitors but at a lower cost, this will immediately result in your achieving a competitive advantage. You could, in effect, charge the same or a slightly lower price and still obtain higher profitability. *

An audit of your competitors' pricing structure is vital to your understanding of the overall market. Even if you are not competing on price you need to understand what the market will accept before you consider your own pricing structure.

Evaluating promotion methods

Once again you must remember that you are still at the audit stage of the marketing planning process. You are not evaluating the promotion methods you intend to use, you are evaluating the promotion techniques that are available to you. It is an established fact that there are numerous promotion methods available but that not all of these will be suited to your business.

In broad terms there are two methods of promotion:

~ impersonal – by far the largest category containing such methods as press, television, cinema and radio advertising, billboard posters, point of sale promotions, and public relations such as sponsorship.

~ personal – direct face-to-face selling, cold calling, telephone selling.

What you need to consider at this stage is which type of promotion technique you may use later. To do that you will need to understand those techniques used by your competitors and, if possible, gauge how successful they are. You also need to consider the actual content of whichever technique they are using. For example, the style and layout of newspaper advertisements, and how often they appear in the press.

Do not forget that your ultimate aim is to have a marketing plan that will give you a competitive advantage. Just because your competitors use a particular promotion technique it does not necessarily follow that it will also be right for your business. As with all aspects of business, there are always new and innovative techniques being developed. If you can use those, rather than the old techniques, it could make your business really stand out above the competition.

It is all a question of considering the options available to you and defining in broad terms the ones that suit your business. For example, you may consider that a mixture of television, radio and press advertisements are best suited to your business. At this stage you will not be deciding on either the content or the timing of such adverts. *

Being in the right place

A successful marketing plan involves having the right products in the right place, at the right time, and also in the right quantity. Very often the last two components are forgotten when the marketing audit is undertaken. In essence then the whole question of place relates to a good overall distribution management system.

Dealing with these three components in order, firstly the physical location of the business. As an extreme example there is little point in considering opening a high-class restaurant in the middle of a remote trading estate. On the other hand, a fast food outlet at the same location, only open for breakfast and lunch, could gain exceptional business in the absence of competition.

If your business offers products or services to the market direct then the question of

The questions that need to be answered are what promotion techniques your competitors are using, and why. You can then decide on your own promotion techniques, but remember they must effectively target your chosen customers.

location will be very important. You will need to establish that wherever you propose to locate, it will be convenient for your customers. You may need, for example, to give consideration to such factors as sufficient parking facilities, especially if the products that you offer are either bulky or heavy. This may even prompt the question of whether or not you need to establish a delivery service.

If on the other hand your products are to be offered on an indirect basis, for example by mail order, the question of location will be less important. It may be that easy access to a main post office will be of more importance to you.

Having your products available at the right time and in the right quantity will affect your business regardless of whether you are selling direct or indirectly. If your products are not available to your customers it is more than likely that they will seek a substitute product from one of your competitors. This is an extremely important factor for a small retailer. Customer loyalty can be very fickle and once they have tried a competitor they may choose to use them in preference to you. *

Summary points

★ Segment your customers and markets into distinctive groups in order that you can be clear of the needs and wants of each segment.

★ Define your products carefully in terms of where they are in the lifecycle process but do not forget also to consider their ongoing profitability.

★ Look at the products offered by your competitors and define them in the same way as you do your own. This will enable you to assess the pricing trends in the market.

★ Do not restrict your evaluation of potential promotion techniques to those used by your competitors. Using innovative or different promotion techniques could give you a competitive advantage.

The demise of many 'corner shops' has come about as the result of a downward spiral. As sales diminished so too did stock levels, resulting in even lower sales and stock levels. Sooner or later the inevitable closure of the shop would follow.

★ Look at all aspects of location, not just the physical premises from which you trade. Your products must be in the right place, at the right time, and in the right quantity.

3 Establishing Your Marketing Objectives

You need to establish where you want to be in the future. Only then can you decide how you are going to get there.

In this chapter four things that really matter:

~ **Using a SWOT analysis**
~ **Using a PESTE analysis to understand your environment**
~ **Understanding the alternatives using an Ansoff matrix**
~ **Establishing your unique selling point**

In Chapter 1 it was strongly emphasised that your marketing objectives must also relate to your overall business objectives. Now that you have completed the marketing audit you can use the information gained to formulate your marketing objectives. This is the second vital stage in the marketing planning process. You have already established where you are in terms of the market, what you must now decide is where you want to be in the future.

Remember the lesson in Chapter 1 – be SMART. You also need to build on your strengths in the market and exploit the opportunities available to you. By the same token, you must counter the threats in the market and minimise your weaknesses. There are a number of tools that you can use when establishing your marketing objectives, for example, both SWOT and PESTE analyses will assist you in this process. *

Is this you?

I already have clear objectives, I want to increase my sales by 10%. • This section isn't really relevant to me. • Why should I complete a SWOT analysis for every product – surely I need to look at my business as a whole? • What relevance is the environment to my marketing? • A unique selling point just sounds like more marketing jargon to me.

* The end result must be marketing objectives that are consistent and compatible with the overall strategic direction of your business.

Using a SWOT analysis

SWOT is the acronym for Strengths, Weaknesses, Opportunities and Threats. A SWOT analysis makes you think about the positive sides of your existing or proposed business as well as the negative aspects. It will summarise all the information you have gained from your marketing audit and should also be concise. Of prime importance is that it should be totally honest. *

Conducting a SWOT analysis involves the construction of a non-financial balance sheet. The analysis is undertaken using a grid to consider how you will match the strengths to the opportunities and how you will overcome the weaknesses and threats. The strengths and opportunities will be listed in the left-hand columns and will be represented by existing or potential assets. The weaknesses and threats will be listed in the right-hand columns and these will be represented by existing or potential liabilities.

* It is insufficient merely to extol your strengths and the opportunities available to you. You must recognise the threats and weaknesses in the market if you are to deal effectively with them.

Strengths – something that you are doing right or are good at. It may be a skill, a competence or a competitive advantage that you have over rivals. Questions to ask: *What are your advantages?* *What do you do well?*	Weaknesses – something that you lack or do poorly when compared to rivals. A condition that puts you at a disadvantage. Questions to ask: *What could be improved?* *What is done badly?* *What should be avoided?*
Opportunities – a realistic avenue for future growth in the business. Something to be used to develop a competitive advantage. Questions to ask: *What are the market trends?* *How can they be exploited?* *What chances are there for me?*	Threats – a factor that you may or may not have control over that could lead to a decline in business. Questions to ask: *What is your competition doing?* *What obstacles do you face?* *What effect will a new entrant to your market have?*

The key points to remember when using a SWOT analysis are:

~ Build on strengths.

~ Resolve weaknesses.

~ Exploit opportunities.

~ Avoid threats.

The SWOT analysis should give you a clear idea of how your business is different from your competitors' both in terms of the market and your products. Having segmented your market and customers within the marketing audit, if you think it necessary you should also prepare an independent SWOT analysis for each segment.

It is important that you understand that your products or services could fall within different segments of the SWOT analysis. Some could be seen as strengths or opportunities for your business. Others could be weaknesses or threats when compared to your competitors'. *

* Make sure that you compare your SWOT analysis to the results you obtained in Chapter 2 when you classified your products using the BCG matrix.

Using a PESTE analysis to understand your environment

There are many factors in the market environment that could impact upon your business and a PESTE analysis is designed to provide a focused framework to assist you in establishing your objectives. It will take the results of your marketing audit and place them in a logical format to ensure that you have considered all of the factors that could affect your market:

P – Political
E – Economic
S – Social
T – Technological
E – Environmental

Political forces can have a direct impact on all markets. Examples of these would be health and safety legislation governing conditions in the workplace and consumer protection legislation covering labelling and packaging. This can be a very important area. Changes in legislation covering the way in which businesses trade can be very costly and in some cases could wipe out your market entirely. A good example is the recent changes in the sale of duty free goods. Whilst for some companies this change was an obvious threat to their business, for others it provided many opportunities.

Economic forces include the effects of inflation and interest and exchange rates. With the development of the Single European Market, even if you do not export any goods or services you may face increasing competition from firms within Europe.

Consider carefully the economic trends within the UK. For example, if interest rates rise will this affect the spending habits of your customers? Can increased costs be passed on or is your market price sensitive?

Social forces include the consideration of changing demographic trends in your customer base and the changing social climate in different parts of the country. They will also include other factors. Changes in consumer life-styles for example, together with the general increase in the average age of the population and housing trends. You should already have considered these factors during the segmentation of your existing and potential customers. What you must now ensure is that your objectives are established to enable you to target the right customers.

Technological forces have been one of the most important factors affecting businesses over the last decade. The development of information technology has impacted on the ways in which business is conducted – for example, the use of faxes and e-mail, and, of course, the opportunities now created by the Internet.

For many businesses the use of the Internet as a marketing tool is little understood and certainly not appreciated. For all businesses, whatever their market, the Internet can be a very efficient marketing tool, creating world-wide sales opportunities for even small, one employee style businesses. *

* You must consider the use of the latest available technology, regardless of your field of business.

The impact of a business on the environment

must be considered as a separate issue when establishing your marketing objectives. Many businesses are now adopting environmentally friendly products which compete against more traditional products that are not produced in such an environmentally friendly manner. For example, some companies avoid animal testing in the manufacture of cosmetics. There can be no doubt that there is a shifting emphasis for people to purchase products that are environmentally friendly, and again, this could be either a threat or an opportunity for you.

In summary, a PESTE analysis will provide you with a wider perspective on the future marketing objectives for your business. The key word is 'future'. Unlike the SWOT analysis that concentrates on the present, a PESTE analysis must be forward looking based on existing knowledge. It is in this way that you can establish objectives that will either counter the threats that you will face in the market or exploit the opportunities that you will find.

Understanding the alternatives using an Ansoff matrix

Igor Ansoff is a Russian-born pioneer of strategic management and corporate planning. Ansoff is also the strategist who first identified the fact that competitive advantage in a market was an essential element of the planning process. This important aspect of marketing is considered in detail in the next section.

The Ansoff matrix defines two key factors for marketing: what is sold and who it is sold to. It therefore relates only to products and markets and gives you four alternative courses of action when considering your primary objectives:

~ selling existing products to existing markets

~ extending existing products into new markets

~ developing new products for existing markets

~ developing new products for new
   markets.

These four options are set out in a matrix
that plots your existing and potential
products against your existing and potential
markets as follows:

	Present Products	New Products
Present Market	Market Penetration	Product Development
New Markets	Market Extension	Diversification

You can now start thinking about your
marketing objectives by using the Ansoff
matrix in conjunction with the analysis of
your products and markets that you
completed using the BCG matrix. You can
also consider a further option relating to
both your products and your markets –
withdrawal. This will generally involve
products that you have designated as 'Dog'
although in some cases it might also include
'Question Marks'.

However, do take heed of the advice given previously. Withdrawal of a product from your product range, or withdrawal from a market, should only happen under exceptional circumstances. These could include situations where you have a weak competitive position or where the associated costs and risks leave a product or market unprofitable.

When establishing your marketing objectives it is also useful to consider Ansoff's definition of the three essential elements of an objective:

1. The particular attribute that is chosen as a measure of efficiency

2. The yardstick or scale by which the attribute is measured

3. The particular value on the scale which the firm seeks to attain.

The above reinforces the SMART criteria set out in Chapter 1 that looked at the differences between business objectives and

The important point to try to focus on is that your competitive advantages must be sustainable. It is essential therefore when you are setting your objectives, based on competitive advantage, that you also consider cost effectiveness and overall profitability. To establish the relationships between benefits to the customer and costs to you, you should consider these four alternative scenarios:

~ low cost to you – low benefit to your customers

~ high cost to you – low benefit to your customers

~ low cost to you – high benefit to your customers

~ high cost to you – high benefit to your customers.

From these options it should be obvious that the competitive advantages that are most cost effective to you, whilst at the same time offering high benefits to your customers,

should be the ones on which you
concentrate your marketing efforts.

Summary points

★ Be honest with yourself when you
  complete your SWOT analysis.

★ Ensure that you assess your marketing
  environment correctly. Changes in the
  market can be costly if you are not
  prepared for them.

★ Use the Ansoff matrix, in conjunction with
  the BCG matrix, when considering your
  primary marketing objectives. You must
  establish what you will sell and to whom.

★ Establish your unique selling points and
  make sure that your customers will see the
  clear benefits of purchasing from you.

Formulating Your Marketing Strategy

Knowing where you want to be is one thing – Establishing the strategies to actually get there is the most difficult part.

In this chapter five things that really matter:

~ **Defining your Critical Success Factors (CSF)**

~ **Managing your product portfolio and lifecycle**

~ **Establishing the right place**

~ **Selecting your promotion techniques**

~ **Deciding on distribution methods**

Deciding on the appropriate marketing strategy is critical to your marketing plan. Your strategy can only be defined after extensive research into the market in order to establish what your customers want. Once you have that information you can then decide on an effective means of meeting that demand. It all revolves around the marketing mix, which is the combination of strategies in respect of product, price, promotion and place.

It is essential that your overall strategy balances the marketing mix exactly. Getting it wrong in one of these key areas could mean overall failure of your strategy. For example, you will fail if you attempt to compete on price when the quality of the product is actually the main consideration for the consumer.

You must also consider whether your strategy is feasible and how it will be implemented. There is little point in formulating a strategy that is incapable of being implemented.

Is this you?

The only factor critical to me is that I need to make money • I only have one product so I don't need to worry about product portfolio and lifecycle. • Price decisions will be easy, I'll just undercut the competition. • All I need to do for promotion is advertise in the local paper. • Distribution methods don't apply to me, I'm in a service industry.

Defining your Critical Success Factors (CSF)

Within all markets there are a number of factors that will be critical to your success. You must address these factors when formulating your strategy if you are to succeed. Under normal circumstances the number of critical success factors will not normally exceed five, although you must understand that there could be secondary factors that will contribute to your success.

All of these critical success factors should have been established during your research and now it is time to prioritise them. Examples of critical success factors could include delivery times, speed of service, quality of the product and competitive pricing. In many ways they will also link up with the competitive advantages that you have established in Chapter 3. *

* Once you have defined the factors critical to your success it is important that you then measure your own performance in these factors relative to your competitors.

The way to do this is to weight each factor out of a total of 100 in terms of how critical it is. You then allocate a score out of ten for your own performance and that of your competitors. It is vitally important that you be totally objective when allocating a score. As an example, you may consider that there are three critical success factors; the first is weighted at 50, the second at 30, and the third at 20.

Once you have allocated a weighting to the factor you then multiply that weighting by the score that you have allocated for performance. This will give you a total score that can be used as a measure of success.

CSF	Weighting	Your Performance		Competitor's Performance	
		Score	Measure	Score	Measure
1	50	8	400	7	350
2	30	5	150	7	210
3	20	6	120	5	100
	100	19	670	19	660

As you can see from the above example, on the basis of the pure scores that have been allocated, both you and your competitor are exactly the same. Taking the weighting of the factors into account, however, you have a marginal competitive advantage. If you find that you are scoring yourself low on the most important factors and high on the least important factors then you obviously need to adopt a strategy that will improve your score on the most important factors. Using this system will help you concentrate your efforts and therefore your strategy on what your customers consider to be important.

Using the same example above you can see that if you improved your score in the second critical success factor to match that of your competitor this would in fact, put you in an overall stronger competitive position. Instead of scoring 150 you would score 210 for this factor, thereby increasing your total score to 730 compared with your competitor's score of 660. *

* Critical success factors will vary from industry to industry and from market to market and there can be no clear formula as to what will be most important for you. You will have to draw on the results of your research and establish your strategy in order to focus on the factors that are critical to your business.

Managing your product portfolio and lifecycle

In Chapter 2 you looked at the use of the BCG matrix to define your product portfolio. You now need to use that information to define your product management strategy. Using the Ansoff matrix from Chapter 3 you will have four options when constructing your product strategy that will also consider your product portfolio and lifecycle:

~ existing products in existing markets

~ existing products in new markets

~ new products in existing markets

~ new products in new markets.

If you attempt to use the BCG matrix to establish your product portfolio and lifecycle strategy it is important that you understand the weaknesses of using it for this purpose. The BCG matrix should only be seen as a guide to classification of your products and not necessarily as an indicator of any future strategy that you should take. There are a number of reasons for this:

~ The matrix fails to take into account your competitor's position relative to the demand for your own products. You may have a significant market share but still have unused spare capacity for production. This means that you cannot take advantage of economies of scale unless demand for your product increases and so, for the moment at least, profit margins could be low.

~ The matrix does not take any account of the strength of your competitors and therefore your 'Star' products may have low profit margins as a result of the high costs of promotion. This could mean that sustaining your 'Stars' in the market could be difficult unless you can increase market share relative to that of your competitors.

~ Too much reliance may be placed on 'Cash Cows' which, because of their nature, are in a low growth market. If the market demand shifts in emphasis and these products decline in popularity, a significant income for your business could be removed overnight. Remember, your product may be the best in the market but if someone else produces something better, or cheaper, you could lose market share. As an example, consider the developments in the vacuum cleaner market over the last ten years and how the new companies, such as Dyson, have taken a substantive market share.

~ The matrix ignores relative profit margins that can also be a factor in market share. You could be selling a product in a specialised niche market with low sales but with a high profit margin. This product could actually be classified by the BCG matrix as a 'Dog' and yet, in real cash terms, it is a high earner for your business. It is therefore important to balance the classification of your products with their margin of profitability. A low sales volume with a high level of profit will have the same effect as a high level of sales at low profit margins.

When considering the strategy relating to your products you must remember that risk should be balanced by reward. A strategy of introducing new products into new markets is measurably riskier than increasing market penetration of existing products in the existing market. By the same token, you cannot afford to do nothing. Sooner or later your existing products will lose demand and you must therefore have a strategy of continuous development for the future.

Your products are the backbone of your business. Unless you sell what customers want, as opposed to what you think they want, you will fail. You must have products that can be developed to meet the changing demand of the market.

Establishing the right price

From the outset do not make the mistake of considering your pricing structure in isolation from the other factors within the marketing mix. Another common mistake is to think that only low prices are competitive, when in fact all pricing policies are competitive.

Taking all of the marketing mix factors together, if your products are of poor quality, are unavailable when they are wanted or your customer service is lacking, no amount of price cutting will make customers buy your products. All of the above is closely related to the unique selling points of your products that by definition cannot be offered by your competitors. *

* If you are of the opinion that you can only compete on price then you are leaving yourself with a strategy that has very few options.

Setting the right price for each of your products can be a difficult exercise because there are so many factors to be taken into account. In simple terms there will probably never actually be one right price but more often a range of pricing options. At the lower end will be the marginal cost of the product beneath which you cannot afford to sell. At the higher end will be the price above which your customers will refuse to purchase from you. *

You will also need to consider profit when constructing your pricing strategy, and to a large extent this will be affected by your projected sales turnover. Within these calculations you will need to take account of both fixed and variable costs. Fixed costs are those costs that are incurred in running your business and which are unrelated to production, for example, the cost of renting your premises. Variable costs are those costs directly related to the cost of production, for example, the raw materials that you use.

Using this information you can then construct a chart to give you the break-even point of your business using a range of pricing options. The key point to remember is that your marketing strategy must include the provision of profits at some stage. That does not mean, however, that you must

• *You will need to balance your price somewhere between these two points.*

always decide on a price that makes a profit.

You may consider initially that market share is more important to you and therefore adopt a price that will effectively buy you that share. Having gained market share you can then increase price accordingly, which will mean increasing overall profitability. As an alternative, if your product is a new invention, you may charge a high price initially, thereby creating a small market niche, and once established reduce the price to gain a larger market share.

As an example of this strategy of charging a high price initially, consider the prices of those products that used micro-processors when they were first introduced. They were extremely expensive. Now that there are many more companies operating in this market, prices have had to come down. Consider this phenomenon in the light of the unique selling point. The initial technology is now no longer unique and as a result, companies are having to compete on terms other than price. *

Purchase decisions by customers are often unrelated to price, and in some cases a high price may indicate higher quality. Think about your own purchases – do you always choose to buy the cheapest option?

Selecting your promotion techniques

In many ways this is the most critical part of your marketing strategy. Communication with your potential customers is vital. You could have the greatest product in the world which everyone needs, but unless they know you have it for sale, they cannot purchase it.

There are no prescriptive promotional techniques that will be suitable for all businesses. The promotion options are virtually limitless and in many ways your strategy will be relative to the budget that you can afford. This is considered in the next chapter, but for the time being you need to choose the advertising mediums that are most appropriate for your business.

If they are to succeed, the promotion techniques that you adopt as part of your marketing strategy must be capable of giving the right information to the right people. When considering your strategy you therefore need to think about:

~ Who your potential customers are

~ What will motivate them to make a purchase

~ How your product matches what they want or need.

From this you will see that your promotion techniques form only a small part of your communication strategy to your customers. Everything about your business, from the products you have, the packaging you use, the sales and after-sales service available, the price, the delivery arrangements, and even your complaint-handling procedures, all send a message to your customers.

At this stage you will recognise that the promotion of your business must bring together the other elements of the marketing mix in order to convert potential customers into purchasers. It is therefore important that you get your message right first time.

In this respect you can use the mnemonic AIDAS:

~ Attract – attract your customers' attention

to generate

~ Interest – you must gain your customers' interest to generate a

~ Desire – you must have something that they want which will make them take

~ Action – your customers must make a purchase and be

~ Satisfied – the ultimate aim, customer satisfaction to make them come back.

This final component, customer satisfaction, is the most important. Nothing will harm your marketing strategy more than a dissatisfied customer. *

*It is a fact that negative publicity travels faster than positive publicity through word of mouth. Just think how many times you have encountered this yourself when a friend has complained about a particular business.

For this reason it is essential that you establish a strategy for two-way communication with your customers as part of your promotion techniques. It is far better for you to have a complaints department that deals effectively with customer complaints because this then gives you information you can use to improve your customers' satisfaction.

To give a personal example, I used the services of a well-known tyre dealer to change some tyres on my car. The next day I discovered that the fitter had not replaced the wheel trim correctly and as a consequence it had been lost somewhere on the road. The dealer had a specific telephone number for complaints which I subsequently used and explained my problem. Without any hesitation the company agreed to pay for a replacement wheel trim. Despite this problem I would obviously use them again because they dealt efficiently with my complaint. More importantly for them, I then told all my friends about the high quality of customer service they offered. *

The key to a successful promotion strategy is to tell the right people about your products. In order to do that you need to know which people want your products. The correct use of the marketing mix is essential.

Deciding on distribution methods

The question of distribution method does not relate solely to location but includes how and when your products will be offered. Distribution management is all about solving the three core issues:

~ being in the right place

~ at the right time

~ with the right quantity of products.

The decisions that you take in formulating your strategy will depend on your type of business. Different considerations will obviously apply depending on whether you are a service business, a retailer or a manufacturer. Invariably you will need to focus on the characteristics of the market in which you operate and, if necessary, the number of potential customers within your catchment area.

The choice of distribution methods can therefore be extremely difficult, although the final decision must relate to your overall objectives and strategy. The right decision can lead, for example, to increased market penetration or the development of new markets. In many ways your strategy will also need to consider the distribution methods used by your competitors.

Do not forget the importance of

competitive advantage when deciding your distribution strategy. As an example, consider the opening hours of many small retailers. With the market growth of the large supermarkets, earlier and later opening hours were the only way that the smaller retailers could compete. This offered a clear benefit to customers and was therefore vital to the survival of many of these small retailers. *

Summary points

★ Clearly define your critical success factors and be objective when considering your score as opposed to the score of your competitors.

* Do not just use the obvious distribution methods. The Internet has opened up many new opportunities for small businesses to compete with large multinational companies on a global scale.

★ Make sure you consistently develop your products to ensure that you are prepared for changes in demand in the market.

★ Do not consider the question of price in isolation. It must be considered as part of the overall marketing mix.

★ Use all available methods of

communication when promoting your business to your customers. Do not forget the importance of dealing positively with customer complaints, as your customers will be telling you what they want.

★ Remember the key points of distribution. You must be in the right place, at the right time, with the right quantity of products.

5 Bringing it all Together

Keep up to date with your market and your competitors.
You will then find more opportunities to improve your performance.

In this chapter four things that really matter:
~ **Establishing your marketing budget**
~ **Writing the marketing plan**
~ **Reviewing your performance**
~ **Staying ahead of the competition**

The whole process of marketing must be ongoing on a day-to-day basis if you are to succeed. Any competitive advantage that you have can be either quickly eroded by imitation or improved upon by a competitor.

Having considered your marketing strategy and written your marketing plan, you must revise it on a regular basis. This will ensure that you actually are meeting your objectives and it will also give you the chance to update your marketing audit. It is vitally important that you stay up to date with what is happening in the market if you are to meet the changing demands of your customers.

Remember the golden rules in marketing – you must have a competitive advantage, offering customers a product that they need. You must be able to supply that product at the right price, in the right place, and in the right quantity. Only by constantly reviewing your own performance, as well as your competitors', can you stay ahead of the competition. *

Is this you?

I don't need a separate budget for my marketing, I'll spend whatever I need to spend. • Writing a marketing plan is just the same as writing a business plan, isn't it? • I spent enough time doing the research and writing the plan, I don't have any time to review it until next year. • Nobody can compete with me, my competitive advantage

The secret of success is to know something nobody else knows. (Aristotle Onassis)

is absolutely unique in the market.

Establishing your marketing budget

Whatever the size of your business it is essential that you allocate a specific budget for marketing. All too often this is seen as just another business expense and treated accordingly on an *ad hoc* basis. Marketing is a key factor of your success and it is important that you recognise this fact.

It is impossible to set clear guidelines on the amount of funding that you should apportion to marketing. It will obviously depend on the size and nature of your business. The amount must be sufficient to meet the promotion strategy that you have formulated but, by the same token, it must be reasonable in terms of your overall business costs.

As an example, if you are considering a marketing budget which amounts to 40% of your projected annual sales turnover, this is probably unreasonable. If, on the other hand,

competitive advantages and the marketing strategies that you propose to use. You will understandably not wish for any of this sort of information to be made available to your competitors.

A good marketing plan will take all the elements of your audit, rationalise your business objectives and then provide a clear outline of your marketing strategies. If you have a number of different products it may even be necessary to segment them and write a marketing plan for each product group. If you deal in a number of different, wide and diverse markets it may also be necessary to write a different marketing plan for each market segment if they are wide and diverse.

The actual content of your marketing plan will vary according to your individual circumstances. The important thing to remember is that it should be extremely comprehensive and yet, at the same time, be simple enough to understand. It should also, unlike your business plan, be delegated to just one person to compile. This may be yourself as the entrepreneur or it may be your marketing specialist. This does not mean that you should not seek the views of others when compiling your marketing audit. *

If you are to succeed you will need to understand the market and then establish your marketing objectives and formulate your strategy. Having complete responsibility personally for the marketing plan will also make it easier for you to review. You can take the ongoing feedback from your sales force and your customers and adapt your objectives and strategies accordingly.

The structure of your marketing plan must concentrate throughout on the key components of marketing – customers, products, price, promotion and place. The plan can be organised under the following suggested headings:

~ An outline of your business objectives and mission statement, which set out the goals and targets for your business as a whole.

It is vital that you have as broad an understanding of the market as possible. The key word here is you.

~ The marketing audit, giving details of the structure of the market, the trends within the market and details of market segmentation for all of the key components of the marketing mix.

~ Marketing objectives, covering the components of the marketing mix together with details of your unique selling points and competitive advantage.

~ Marketing strategies that will define your critical success factors, giving details of your strategy for the components of the marketing mix.

~ Resources that will be required to implement the marketing plan both in terms of cash funding and staff.

Unless the plan is communicated effectively to the people who are required to implement it, there will be little chance of success.

Once the marketing plan has been written, make sure it is shared with all employees. They must understand what it is you wish to achieve and what strategies you propose to adopt to enable you to get there. *

Reviewing your performance

Once you have completed your written marketing plan that is not the end of the marketing process. You must treat marketing as a process along the lines of an ever-spinning wheel – you can never reach the end.

The very moment that you finish researching and writing your marketing plan it will be out of date. Any unique selling point and competitive advantage that you have could have been lost as a result of a change in the market. This important aspect is covered in detail in the next section.

You must put in place a comprehensive process to review all of the elements of your marketing plan. This must cover all of the essential elements of the marketing audit which of necessity will also cover all of your marketing objectives. The SWOT and PESTE analyses must be updated on a regular basis to take account of changes in the market, thus providing you with new opportunities. Remember too that there may well be new threats that you will need to address.

You should also concentrate on the essential components of the marketing mix, not only on an individual basis, but also to ensure that the balance within the mix remains the optimum one for your business. In Chapter 4 you looked at the product lifecycle process and how it is important that you identify changes in consumer demand for your products.

As highlighted previously, in order to achieve optimum value for money you should also maintain statistics on which form of promotion technique is bringing you customers. You should also be reviewing your overall promotion strategy. Do not forget that all forms of communication with your customers are important.

Unless you keep abreast with what your customers are demanding from the market you will lose the essential component of marketing. That is the provision of a product that customers either want or need, or both. Changes in demand should not come as a surprise to you as you should be looking for signs well in advance of it actually happening. *

Staying ahead of the competition

The importance of maintaining your unique selling point and competitive advantage through ongoing market intelligence and competitor information is paramount. Up-to-date information about your market will keep you aware of changes or developments that could affect your business. This information may also indicate trends in consumer demand that you can exploit. It could also potentially help you to identify economic trends in the market that could affect the buying habits of your customers.

Market intelligence will enable you to update your sales forecasts on a regular basis and this will also assist you when reviewing your overall strategy. It is also critical that you keep track of your competitors. On an ongoing basis you need to find out what they are doing, what they are charging and any new products they have launched which

Constant review of business performance is essential. Constant review of your marketing plan is critical. If you lose your customers through changes in the market you may well lose your business.

could compete with you. Even if you consider that your product is the best in the market there will always be someone who will try to compete with you on a different factor of the marketing mix.

If you employ sales staff, ensure that they obtain feedback from your customers. It is highly likely that your customers will also be looking at the activities of your competitors and it may be that they can provide you with 'inside' information. For example, it is not unknown for a competitor to approach a customer of a rival firm and offer some form of inducement such as a discount or better credit terms in order to gain their business. Unless you have information on this sort of activity at an early stage you could well find your customer base declining.

Competitive advantage is everything in business. You must retain a unique selling point that will consistently bring you new customers as well as repeat business. The only way you can do this is continually to research the market in order to establish exactly what is happening. *

Information is power and unless you have that power you may miss out on new opportunities available to you in the market. Even worse, you could succumb to new threats in the market that could destroy your business.

Summary points

★ Establish a clearly defined budget for your marketing. Marketing is a key component of your business activity and you must allocate sufficient resources to carry it out.

★ Ensure your marketing plan is comprehensive yet simple to understand with clear objectives and strategies. Communicate it effectively to all staff and make sure they understand the future direction of your business and how you propose to reach your destination.

★ Review your marketing plan on a regular basis, at least monthly, preferably weekly. The faster you can respond to changes in the market, the better your chances of success.

★ Always maintain a unique selling point and competitive advantage. Without these there is nothing to differentiate you from your competitors and therefore no compelling reason why customers should purchase your product.

Appendix
Sample Marketing Plan Template

Section One –
Contact details

Under normal circumstances a marketing plan will only be written for internal use within the business because it will contain sensitive trading information. If, however, it is to be exhibited externally it should contain clear details of the company or trading name, the registered and trading address and contact name with telephone and fax numbers together with e-mail and web site address if appropriate. It should also contain details of any relevant advisors e.g. accountant, lawyer or consultant.

Section Two –
Market Analysis

This section will segment both the market and the potential customer. It is essential that you categorise your market and your customers into groups that contain the same broad characteristics.

There are four rules to follow when segmenting your market and customers:

1. Segments must be of a suitable size in comparison with the overall market.

2. The customers within each segment must be similar in nature, but at the same time be entirely distinct from other customers.

1. The customers within the segment must be accessible.

This part of your marketing plan is the most substantive and will require a substantial amount of time and research.

Section Three – Competitor Analysis

Competition to your business could come in four different ways:

1. Direct – from businesses that offer the same products or services as you in the same market.

your market

3. Industry – from businesses that operate in the same product area but who sell in different markets.

4. Linked – from businesses that offer the same services but deliver in a different manner.

Section Four – Product Analysis

Product analysis is one of the most important parts of your marketing. You need to make sure that the products you offer are actually desired by the potential customer. Unless you have the right products you will have no business.

Section Five – Promotion Analysis

At this stage you need an analysis of the promotion techniques that are available to you. They might be those that you use already or those that are commonly used by your competitors.

Section Six – Place Analysis

Do not make the mistake of thinking that place considerations only relate to your physical location. You need to think of place as being the whole method in which you make your sales, i.e. the whole distribution of your goods or services. In essence it covers the question of having the right products in the right place at the right time.

Section Seven – Marketing Objectives

By this stage you will have gained a significant amount of information about your own, and indeed your competitors' products. The establishment of marketing objectives should therefore be relatively easy. Remember that marketing objectives can only relate to products and markets. In addition, you have only four options when you decide on what they will relate to.

~ Selling existing products to existing markets

~ Extending existing products into new markets

~ Developing new products for existing markets

~ Developing new products for new markets

Put your marketing objectives in plain terms, and provide some means of objective measure to enable you to actually establish if they have been achieved. Your marketing objectives must also be consistent with your overall business objectives.

Section Eight – Mission Statement

The mission statement will appear at the start of your marketing plan and should provide details of the focus and purpose of your business.

The mission statement is written in two parts. First outline the industry that you are in and the products or services that you offer. The second part provides core details of the strategies that you will follow to achieve success.

The mission statement must, in usually no more than four or five paragraphs, detail succinctly the whole thrust of your business. It is usually better, therefore, to write it once all the other components of the marketing plan have been written. In this way it will act as a summary of what you propose for the future.

Section Nine – Unique Selling Points

This section will deal exclusively with the competitive advantages that you either have already or those that you propose for the future, your Unique Selling Points, or USPs.

Section Ten – Critical Success Factors

Under normal circumstances the number of Critical Success Factors (CSFs) should not exceed five and for obvious reasons you need to be sure that they are the factors that are of primary importance to the consumer. When you did your research into what consumers want to buy you may have discovered a number of factors that appeared to be of importance. It is, however, likely that some of these factors could be considered as secondary, or possibly linked with other factors that can be grouped together under one heading.

Section Eleven – Product Strategy

This section will outline the products, or services, that are to be offered in the future. This also needs to be linked to the potential customers in the market, in other words what are you going to sell and to whom?

Remember that every product or service is purchased to satisfy a desire or need by the consumer. You need to establish what it is the consumer desires and then describe how you propose to satisfy that desire.

This means that you need to outline the features and benefits of your products. Features are what a product has, and the benefits are what the product does for the consumer. Match the features of your product to the benefits that your customer will get when they purchase it.

Section Twelve – Price Strategy

The overriding factor to consider when setting a price is that your objective must be to make a profit. However, that does not necessarily mean that you must make a profit from the outset. Some pricing strategies could involve a low initial price purely to quickly gain market share. On the other hand, with a totally new and innovative product, your initial strategy may be to charge as high a price as the market will stand.

With that in mind you will appreciate that the price will vary to meet the changing demands of the market. It will also be affected by the supply and demand for the products within the market. The major factors affecting pricing decisions are:

~ Customers

~ Costs

~ Competitors

~ Business Objectives

Section Thirteen – Promotion Strategy

Promotion is about the way in which you communicate with your customers. In plain terms it is saying the right thing to the right people. This means that everything you do, from your stationery and business cards through to the format and presentation of your advertisements, must convey the right message.

The mix of communication strategies that you can use for promotion is virtually endless. The important part is selecting those that will provide you with the most return. Always remember that the most expensive option is not always the best option. Reputation and image also play a large part and these cannot be bought, they have to be earned.

Section Fourteen – Distribution Strategy

Place considerations do not relate solely to physical location. They also relate to how and when your products will be offered. In short, they are the distribution management techniques that you will use to solve three key issues:

~ Being in the right place

~ at the right time

~ with the right amount of products.

Section Fifteen – Management Information System

The very moment that you finish researching and writing your marketing plan, it will be out of date. Any unique selling point and competitive advantage that you have could well be lost as a result of a change in the market. You can only stay ahead of the competition by constantly reviewing the demands of the consumer and the market.

You must now put in place a comprehensive

Management Information System to review all of the elements of your marketing plan. The SWOT and PESTE analyses must be updated on a regular basis to take account of changes in the market, thus providing you with new opportunities. Remember too that there may well be new threats you will need to address.

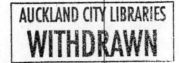